This coloring book belongs to:

_____

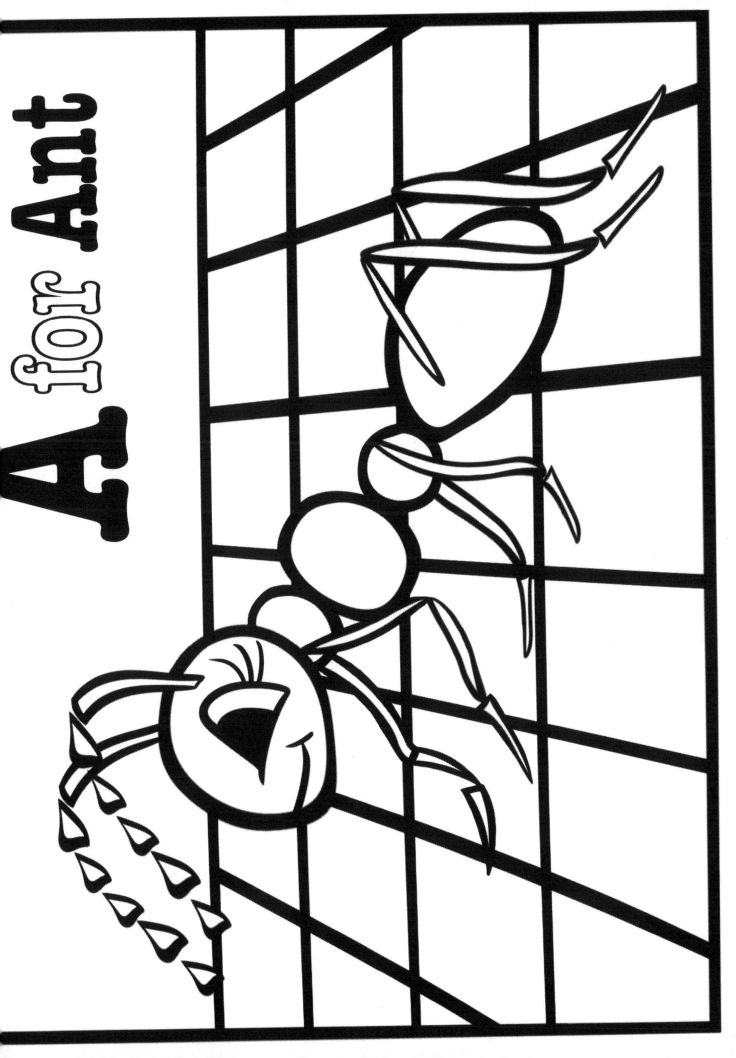

B for Bumble Bee

C for Caterpillar

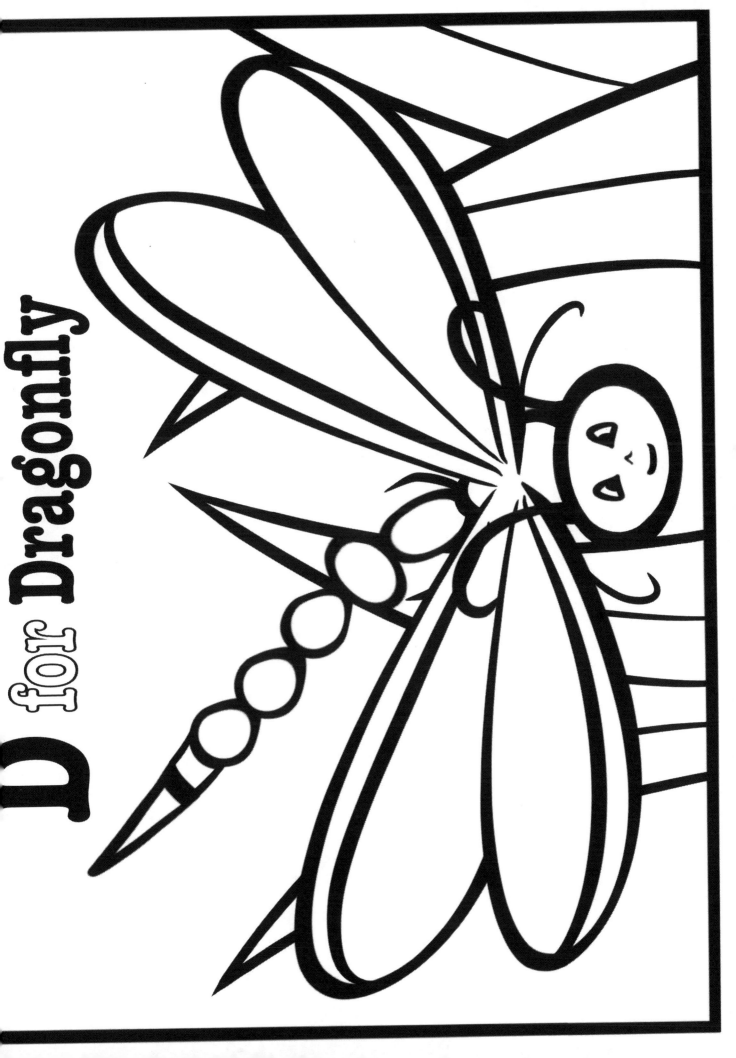

D for Dragonfly

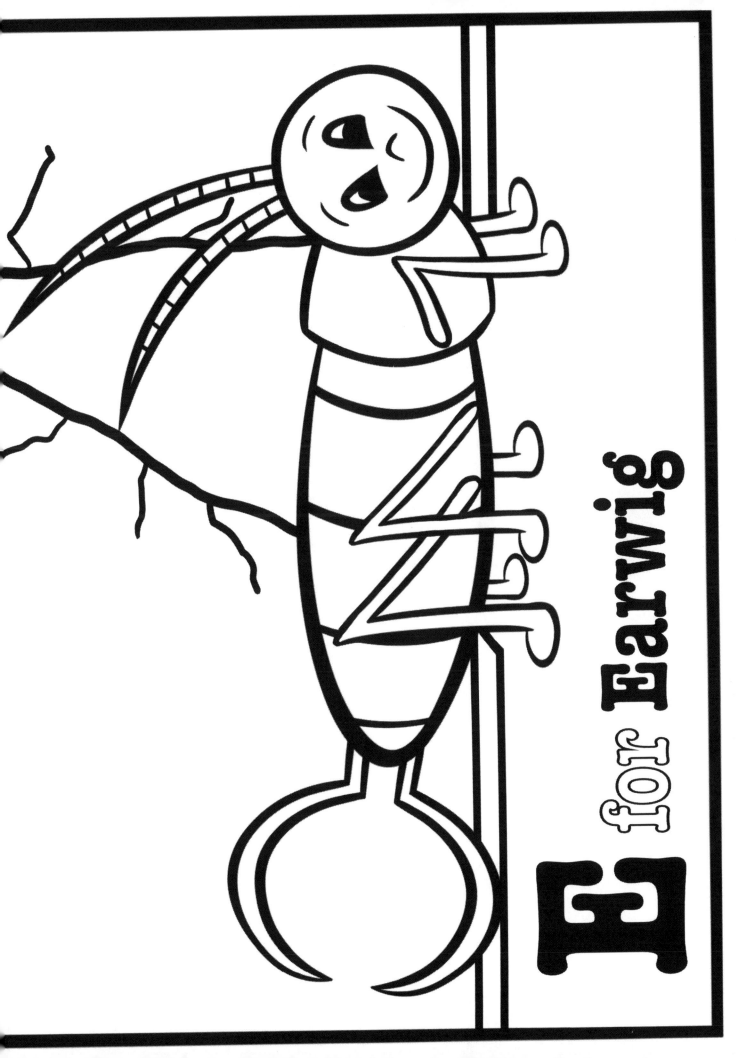

E for Earwig

F for Firefly

G for Grasshopper

H

for House Fly

I for Io Moth

J for June Bug

K for Katydid

L for Ladybug

M for Mosquito

N for Netwing

O for Owlfly

P for Praying Mantis

Q for Queen Butterfly

R for Rhinoceros Beetle

T for Termite

U for **Underwing Moth**

V for Velvet Ant

W for Waterbug

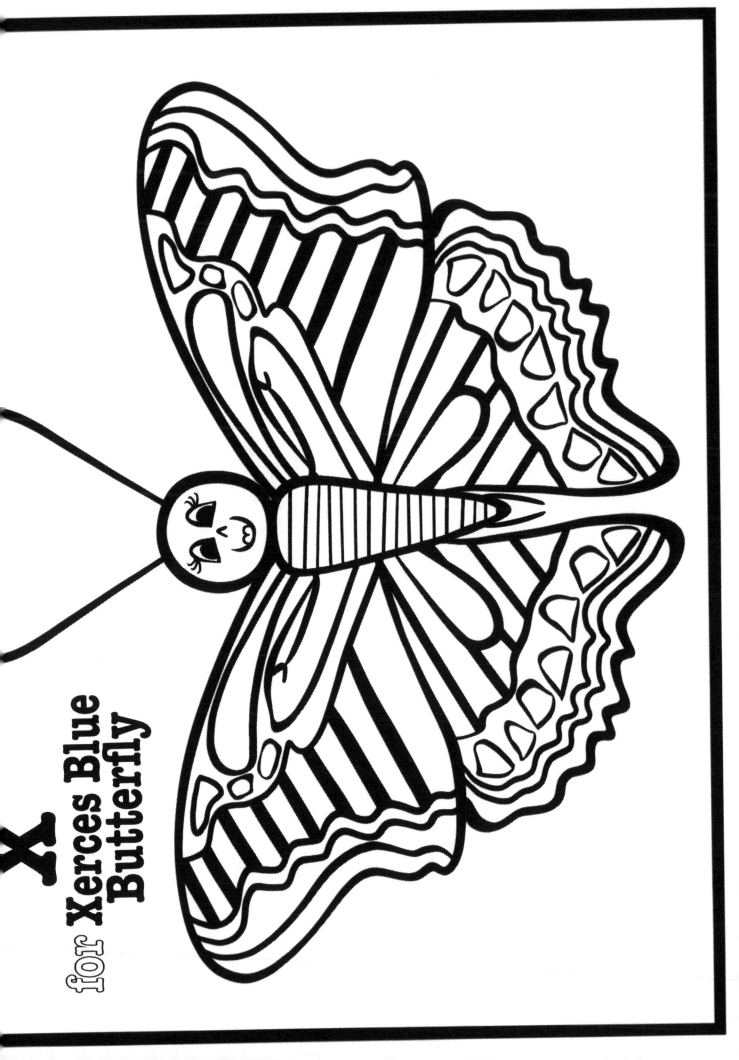

X

for Xerces Blue
Butterfly

Y for Yellow Jacket

Z
for Zebra
Butterfly

Made in the USA
Columbia, SC
11 August 2024

40331234R00030